FALL TENDERLY

Fall Tenderly

Poems
by
SHARI JO LeKANE

Adelaide Books
New York/Lisbon
2018

FALL TENDERLY
Poems
By Shari Jo LeKane

Copyright © by Shari Jo LeKane
Cover design © 2018 Adelaide Books

Published by Adelaide Books, New York / Lisbon
adelaidebooks.org

Editor-in-Chief
Stevan V. Nikolic

All rights reserved. No part of this book may be reproduced in any manner whatsoever without written permission from the author except in the case of brief quotations embodied in critical articles and reviews.

For any information, please address Adelaide Books
at info@adelaidebooks.org
or write to:
Adelaide Books
244 Fifth Ave. Suite D27
New York, NY, 10001

ISBN-10: 1-949180-18-2
ISBN-13: 978-1-949180-18-3

Printed in the United States of America

Contents

Fall Tenderly 9

The Proposal *10*

Wedding Vow *11*

After Dark *12*

Midnight Affair *13*

Timekeeper's Waltz *14*

Harmonious Mix *15*

I Am Woman *16*

Bandit of Love *17*

The Call of a Stranger *18*

You Cannot Live Here Anymore *19*

The Bitter to the Sweet *20*

Have You Seen My Gray Today? *22*

Hang *23*

The Humanitarian *24*

November Grey *25*

Migraine *26*

Beyond Love *27*

Pain *28*

Garden of Earthly Delights *29*

Desert with No End *30*

My Disease *31*

Nightmare *32*

Farewell, Miss Saigon *33*

Sand in My Shoes *34*

The Struggle *35*

Now That You're Gone *36*

How Did You Know? *37*

In the Rear-View Mirror *38*

Being is Becoming *39*

Silver Lining *41*

My Drug Is True *43*

For Still She Waves *44*

Thank You for Sharing *45*

Sands of Tim *46*

What if Jesus Flew for United? *47*

FALL TENDERLY

Empty Nest *48*

I Remembered *49*

Cinderella *51*

The Prince Is Having A Ball *52*

Autumnal Equinox *53*

Only in October *54*

Starry Night *55*

Holy Night *56*

Dance of the Boughs *57*

Wintery Silence *58*

Perpetual Motion *61*

Once in a Blue Moon *62*

Monarch *63*

Double Exposure *64*

February *65*

Doldrums *67*

The Lorax on Westgate *68*

Spring Equinox *70*

About the Author *73*

Acknowledgements *75*

Publishing Credits *77*

Fall Tenderly

Amidst the soft and muted light, they glowed like burning embers,
dancing in the wind around the tombstones, as I recall;
it was an autumn rainbow of red and orange
and gold to be remembered.
Fall tenderly like the leaves brushing against the graveyard wall.

You were placing flowers on a grave and you had been crying,
mourning someone very dear, and you looked so very small
in this granite-filled lot of incendiary leaves and so much dying.
Fall tenderly in my arms and make me stand up straight and tall.

When you gently took my arm, it was an electric kind of sizzle,
and the rush of your touch made all of my skin crawl;
there were tears in our eyes as they met, and it began to drizzle.
Fall tenderly into the night as the whispering raindrops call.

I don't care about the past, I no longer have misgivings;
I am here for the present, for now, and I am trying to stall,
because life is for us, it is for those who are here and still living.
Fall tenderly into my heart and promise me your all.

The Proposal

There's a moment in life when you know that it's right
to pursue a due change in its course.
Furthermore, the confluence of our two lives
brings me to the following proposal.

I've been thinking it over for quite a long time,
and I've come to a brilliant conclusion.
What started as friendship has blossomed into
something greater than I could imagine.

You stirred the very depths of my searching soul
with your strength and compassionate ways.
Your beauty attracts me, I'm under your spell,
and I dream of you day and night.

My feelings have deepened for you, my love,
to the point where I can't live without you.
I envision a life for the two of us, dear,
and I'm willing to make you so happy.

The life I was living before I met you
had no meaning, for now I'm alive.
Darling, my heart is decidedly yours
for the taking, if only you'll have me.

Wedding Vow

The moment I saw you my heart must have known
just how special you are as a friend and a man.
Then, over time as our friendship had grown
we were falling in love as if by nature's hand.

The spark of this romance, divinely inspired,
includes future plans on a journey for two.
Dreams can come true, and for all we've aspired,
I cannot imagine a world without you.

Destiny flutters in anticipation
from heavenly rafters to here and to now.
God is my witness, you're my inspiration;
to you I recite my sincere wedding vow.

I'll cherish you, dear, for the rest of my life,
with you as my husband, and me as your wife.

After Dark

As twilight ascends into tender turquoise,
I stare from my window upon yonder park;
it sweetly reminds me of your taste and noise,
and when we first kissed under stars after dark.

You looked in my eyes, I saw passion reflected;
the rush of your touch was electricity
as you brought my face closer and our lips connected,
so perfectly paired in synchronicity.

Now I adore you, so blessed that you're near me;
I give you my love, you give me all your heart.
I wonder if ever you seem to grow weary,
until we're complete after we've been apart.

Rarely in passing we'll share cross remarks,
but then our lips meet when we greet after dark.

Midnight Affair

Moon flowers bloomed in their translucent glory
against humid darkness. I tasted night air
and inhaled stale smoke as you told me your story
with cool reservation. I tried not to stare.

It started as casual conversation,
but music came on and you asked me to dance
to a slow Latin beat, and without hesitation
I followed your lead in a rhythmic romance.

We swayed to the samba that came from your jeep
when you brought my face closer and gave me a kiss.
It lasted as long as the song, and I deeply
relaxed in your bliss. Should the world end like this?

Dawn woke the birds who sang morning's first prayer
and ushered an end to the midnight affair.

Timekeeper's Waltz

From the very last stroke of the dancing alarm clock,
when dreamscapes are melting to sweet reverie
in the sieve of subconscious where spirits unlock,

there's a synergy building for delivery.
Ushered in fresh like a strong handyman,
with a rustic world view and gestalt bravery,

- Step, two, three, back, two, three – just like Candy land -
If the Lord is deceased, is the Widow endowed?
Gently she rests, singing love to the Ottoman.

Overstuffed daydreams in blue jeans are allowed,
when will this figment assume incarnation -
enrapturing mainstays to lay claim out loud?

Beggarly trust in the evaluation
of romantic love is an eternal plight
for all who may end up in the realization

that time waltzes on in the midst of the fight
while we're dancing on, keeping step, doing right.

Harmonious Mix

Court jester juggles his literary bag of tricks
in the red morning hours; he sonorously sings,
"Will you resuscitate the harmonious mix?"

Blue junkie robs from the graves to get a fix
from a weedling needle, sweet and dirty, it stings.
Court jester juggles his literary bag of tricks.

Green sticks in cars rushing out to hang with cliques
smell of sweat and perfume that youthfulness brings.
"Will you resuscitate the harmonious mix?"

Dance an orange tango - Spanish plaza made of bricks,
to a local Mariachi, when the clock tower rings.
Court jester juggles his literary bag of tricks.

Drum perfect time for the band with purple sticks
as chicks with flowing hair (no underwear) are smiling.
"Will you resuscitate the harmonious mix?"

Weak soul lingers Cimarron, so the Grim Reaper picks
on a mellow yellow Sunday, like a field in the Spring.
Court jester juggles his literary bag of tricks,
"Will you resuscitate the harmonious mix?"

I Am Woman

I am Woman with mindset of steel:
forging wheels on the line in a foundry;
breaking ceilings of glass with no boundaries
in the corporate world making deals.

Treating patients so that they may heal;
teaching students with vigor and zeal;
gaining knowledge both complex and sundry;
I am Woman.

Always humble at heart to reveal
to the ones that I love what I feel;
domesticity roles, doing laundry,
solving problems when we're in a quandary,
giving thanks for each day that's been sealed.
I am Woman.

Bandit of Love

The masque is my bandit of love in disguise,
strumming the chords of my finely tuned heartstrings
like Spanish Boleros, with deep gypsy eyes.

Sleek as a jaguar beneath jungle skies
in a nocturnal swing, bringing joy to the willing.
The masque is my bandit of love in disguise.

Exceptional ardor in all exercise
with a sensual rasp in his voice when he sings,
like Spanish Boleros, with deep gypsy eyes.

Why do I cry when I see through these lies?
His frivolous flings are as painful as bee stings.
The masque is my bandit of love in disguise.

To tender caresses and tones he complies,
while passionate pleasures ignite and take wing
like Spanish Boleros, with deep gypsy eyes.

For all who may fall for the bandit, be wise.
To money like honey he clings to these things.
The masque is my bandit of love in disguise
like Spanish Boleros, with deep gypsy eyes.

The Call of a Stranger

Once in a while comes the call of a stranger.
One first reaction is, "Where do I hide?"
Could it be friendly or imminent danger?

Feelings if stress and suspicion abide.
Fight or take flight is a process inherent.
One first reactions is, "Where do I hide?"

Whatever happened to being transparent,
attuned as the new interactions evolve?
Fight or take flight is a process inherent.

Low dialogue helps the stressors dissolve.
A friendly cascade of delight can persuade,
attuned as the new interactions evolve.

Thoughts of the worst are so hard to evade,
but sometimes connections leave feelings of wonder.
A friendly cascade of delight can persuade.

Exercise caution to side-step a blunder.
Sometimes connections leave feelings of wonder.
Once in a while comes the call of a stranger.
It could be friendly or imminent danger.

You Cannot Live Here Anymore

We Wish You a Merry
empty printer cartridge

And a Happy printer alignment
now that your bi-polar disorder
has totally overcome Good Tidings

We Bring Wherever You Are
foregone conclusion should have seen

Good Tidings for Christmas and a

Happy New Year in the Psyche Ward
involuntary admission candy canes
s/he always loved icicle lights
sedation can help but s/he tries to escape

Silver Bells s/he succumbs to the drugs

Hear Them Ring plays along with group

Soon It Will Be graduation day
back on the street to do it all again
but no you cannot live here anymore

The Bitter to the Sweet

No one knows quite what to expect whenever we should meet
as we negotiate the ups and downs of the cyclical bipolar maze.
I only try to just get by the bitter to the sweet.

After all, the manic outbursts are only a temporary phase,
and we certainly know that your lows do
not mean that you are truly lazy,
as we negotiate the ups and downs of the cyclical bipolar maze.

Ironically, you think that everyone has labeled you as crazy,
when in reality, you are the one who lives in the greatest self-denial;
and we certainly know that your lows do
not mean that you are truly lazy.

In fact, a clinical diagnosis does not mean that you are on trial,
and regulation of medications has proven to stabilize your moods;
but in reality, you are the one who lives in the greatest self-denial.

Perhaps you are too young to absorb the
wisdom your experience exudes.
Over time as you mature, you will settle
down and gain more confidence,
and regulation of medications has proven to stabilize your moods.

FALL TENDERLY

For now, the path is ambiguous and left to the fate of providence.
Over time as you mature, you will settle
down and gain more confidence.
No one knows quite what to expect whenever we should meet;
I only try to just get by the bitter to the sweet.

Have You Seen My Gray Today?

Have you seen my gray today?
The melding of darkness and light;
an absence of color at play.

A cameo profile for pay
with stark shades from shadow to bright.
Have you seen my gray today?

Do I know if in daylight I stray?
Or if blindly I melt in the night?
An absence of color at play.

The stupor from nocturnal fray
concussed like a nightmarish bite.
Have you seen my gray today?

Imagine an infinite ray
piercing blackness with one point in sight;
an absence of color at play.

My ship will be sailing away
on horizons that fog and unite.
Have you seen my gray today?
An absence of color at play.

Hang

Your limbs, they sag, like broken hangers,
frosted with icing and powdery snow.

And near your base, decomp is suspended,
a hangover from last summer's vernal growth.

Now fledgling flocks all fluffed and frolicky
hang on, waiting for the promise of spring.

Yet stranger fruit have borne your branches
in hang man days of mobster lynching.

With roots so deep and a reach growing higher,
you are always hanging in a delicate balance.

Though you hang out now in a restful winter sleep,
you always and freely share your many talents.

The Humanitarian

Speaking of literacy, what do you say?
Forests of print rich environments stand,
rooted in language and culture, conveying
the history of knowledge at our command.

Talk of initiative, what do you do?
Keep sense of knowing oneself from within,
and power to take on new challenges, too,
while maintaining confidence; never give in.

Vocalize leadership, what does it take?
Compassion for suffering, those who seek aid;
Love in our hearts for all matters at stake;
Wisdom to guide each decision that's made.

Tell of rewards for a life led this way.
Success breeds success and plants roots that will stay.

November Grey

The Silver Maple leaves look so innocent and cheery
against the November Grey piles of dankness and mold;
now the newly barren branches seem both scarred and weary.

Daylight Savings time has ended, and evenings are dreary.
I look in the mirror and see someone foreign and old.
The Silver Maple leaves look so innocent and cheery.

We rake out the leaves and it makes my eyes teary;
I pick up where the Halloween pumpkin has rolled.
The newly barren branches seem both scarred and weary.

Mr. Hawk perches in the front yard, how rare and eerie
to watch as he hunts his prey both nobly and bold
while the Silver Maple leaves look so innocent and cheery.

Frost soon appears across the lawns and we are leery
to leave precious remnants of summer out in the cold.
The newly barren branches seem both scarred and weary.

We look forward to Holidays that come around yearly .
that begin with these changes that take their strong hold.
The Silver Maple leaves look so innocent and cheery,
and the newly barren branches seem both scarred and weary.

Migraine

The road to recovery is nebulous and long
with glimmers of hope between thunder storms,
yet the twists and turns are like a never-ending song.

From the moment the aura begins to form
and the intense migraine injects its pain
with glimmers of hope between thunder storms,

to the point of being driven totally insane
while waiting for the drugs to take their effect,
and the intense migraine injects its pain.

Only rocking helps, everything else you reject.
So you pick up a pencil and jot down a rhyme
while waiting for the drugs to take their effect,

and a rhyme becomes a terzanelle in little time,
because poetry soothes the pain in the brain.
So you pick up a pencil and jot down a rhyme,

you finish the verse through the haze that remains,
because poetry soothes the pain in the brain.
The road to recovery is nebulous and long,
yet the twists and turns are like a never-ending song.

Beyond Love

Our relationship is heightened to a plane beyond love,
a metaphysical existence far from emotional terrors;
and it satisfies the soul that is elevated above
the mere pleasure of love and its inevitable human errors.

Once upon a time my heart was inextricably intertwined
with your every thought and feeling to the point of preoccupation.
Then I learned the sublime intricacies of
your being, and I am reminded
of how philosophical our exchanges became a matter of vocation.

When I faced life-threatening illness, it
brought about a different life.
We all are affected by this, yet we successfully forge ahead.
There are different ways we handle pain,
and so many forms of strife,
but our moments of joy are jewels, and a humble life we have led.

Through the heartache and ardor, there is so much more, it is true;
life together is truly a blessing, and I am so beyond love with you.

Pain

Pain is nothing more than a wounded lover,
where the heart is but a vulnerable bloom,
from former pleasure trying hard to recover.

Remembering the scent of a faraway perfume
that is oh, so hard, in memory to retrieve,
where the heart is but a vulnerable bloom.

In the depth of darkness, it cannot perceive
the far-gone pleasure of a past holiday
that is oh, so hard, in memory to retrieve.

It is the distant call of a friend to delay
a reunion to some other place unknown,
or the far-gone pleasure of a past holiday.

The pain in its twisted jealousy has shown
the ability to shadow the beauty and reveal
a reunion to some other place unknown

where the ugly fate is finally sealed,
and freedom from hurt is soundly concealed.
Yes, pain is nothing more than a wounded lover,
from former pleasure, trying hard to recover.

Garden of Earthly Delights

Long ago, the heavens did shine so bright
to break through the darkness of particle storms,
and shone upon the Garden of Earthly Delights.

Before then everything was nothing but night
as the elements turned and the Earth was formed,
then long ago, the heavens did shine so bright.

And the miracle of light was a beautiful sight
as it turned the planet into a terrarium of reform,
and shone upon the Garden of Earthly Delights.

Protected from darkness within its orb of might,
it kept its precious consignment safe and warm,
for long ago, the heavens did shine so bright.

And as time passed, more creatures came to light
to inhabit the Earth, while the Sun still adorned
and shone upon the Garden of Earthly Delights.

Then evolved homo sapiens to decide what was right
in the midst of this Eden from which s/he was torn.
Long ago the heavens did shine so bright,
and shone upon the Garden of Earthly Delights.

Desert with No End

I carry my baggage of life without amends,
and all of my earthly delights I relinquish
to eternally cross the desert with no end.

For all of my fraternal acquaintances are offended
that the seven deadly sins ruled me; I was selfish.
Now I carry my baggage of life without amends

There is no concept of family or even friends
in this ghoulish sandstorm where the air is superstitious,
and I eternally cross the desert with no end.

A torturous hope is that the way up ahead will bend
and lead to something other than what is repetitious,
but I carry my baggage of life without amends

It occurs to me that I would like to send
my baggage ahead to make the journey more expeditious,
but I eternally cross the desert with no end.

For those who will come later, let me lend
a bit of advice: live a life that is judicious
or you will carry your baggage of life without amends
and eternally cross the desert with no end.

My Disease

I've been diagnosed with Acromegaly, a terminal disease
that is identified by a pronounced growing malaise
caused by a tumor on the pituitary gland, if you please.

At first in denial, I thought it just a passing phase,
but the headaches lead to bad dreams and hallucinations,
then alcohol and narcotics, and the road to a lifelong craze.

The physical pain exceeded my wildest imagination
as my body evolved and assumed crippling contortions
with the disease, as though expressing physical retaliation.

I underwent brain surgery and gamma knife radiation,
and both left me in a stupefied haze;
but I refused to succumb to spiritual abortion.

Though I was told I might die, or at best, be in a daze,
as you can see, I am a survivor, and I am here, still.
The power of belief and healing never ceases to amaze.

So much of my life is dictated by being ill,
but I am determined to beat this, and I know that I will.

Nightmare

Your wretched smile was ironed on my mind
like an unrecognizable road kill,
and the scream in my throat was too dry to find.

I tried to use every ounce of my will
to wake, but I lay in bed, instead,
like an unrecognizable road kill.

While you crowded your horrors in my head
of painting me in a Hieronymus Bosch,
I did not wake, I lay in bed, instead.

You gave birth from someone missing a crotch
while I ran from the bird man with evil eyes;
you painted me in a Hieronymus Bosch.

With overt disgust I grew to despise;
the fear in the night kept me paralyzed,
but I ran from the bird man with evil eyes.

It was long after dawn when I realized
that the fear in the night kept me paralyzed.
Your wretched smiled was ironed on my mind,
and the scream in my throat was too dry to find.

Farewell, Miss Saigon

After all these fine years of treasures bygone,
the fleet pulls me back to the dungeonous sea.
I bid *sayonara*, and farewell, Miss Saigon.

"Return to the ship," says the captain to me
the night before we were about to set sail;
the fleet pulls me back to the dungeonous sea.

And then there arose such a terrible gale
that had the crew worried for our success
the night before we were about to set sail.

We all came aboard with anxiety and stress
as the sky told the story of an angry storm
that had the crew worried for our success.

The wind blew the sails 'till they burst into form
while the ship rolled asunder on mounting waves
as the sky told the story of an angry storm.

We knew we were headed for watery graves
while the ship rolled asunder on mounting waves.
After all these fine years of treasures bygone,
I bid *sayonara*, and farewell, Miss Saigon.

Sand in My Shoes

Was it only yesterday that we walked along the shore
collecting seashells and mangroves among the wild sea grapes
in the golden September sun of Melbourne's ocean door?

Feeling white sand in my shoes along the foamy, wavy seascapes,
and Emmanuel went in the water and lost his sunglasses.
"A sacrifice to the Gods," so he said, as they escaped.

Then Peanut and Artie made several quick passes
between the beach and the water and into the waves,
but their favorite spot was tent-side where they liked to relax.

Now Nikia knows ocean and plant life, and she often raves
of the initiatives she undertakes to insure their good health,
like the clean beach programs to stop litterbugs that she staves!

Artie and Nikia ran together in a marathon with great stealth
for the annual Turtle Krawl that generated much good news.
I realize how much their shared life has created a great wealth.

So whenever I grow weary of these St. Louis Blues,
I always remember when I got sand in my shoes.

The Struggle

The trouble with pain is the struggle with time:
quite often they run infinite, parallel lines
that never intersect, but they increasingly climb
in intensity and fail to forgivingly align.

Without some serious forms of intervention,
it would be impossible to avoid suicidal tendencies;
but the upshot of taking all these medications
is an overwhelming realization of drug dependency.

There never will be any certifiable guarantee
that the drugs will always do the trick.
A storm can come along and send you on a pain spree,
and no kind of drug can give you a fix.

Negotiating the struggle to manage chronic pain
is a full-time job for the major leagues;
it consumes every moment in order to remain sane,
and it causes high incidence of combat fatigue.

Now That You're Gone

Now that you're gone,
I try to show courage
and present a strong face
to the world on my own.

Now that you're gone,
I seem to forget
all the frivolous drivel
that drove me insane.

Now that you're gone,
I want to remember
particular nuances
that I adored.

Now that you're gone,
I need to look forward
to new independence
and us being friends.

How Did You Know?

How did you know when I needed a friend?

A kindly soul to guide me,
an ear to listen,
your gentle nods,
kind eyes to see,
your nonjudgmental responses.

How did you know?

You must be a truly dear friend
if you can read me like a book.
I want you to know how grateful I am
to be blessed with a dear friend like you.

Thank you for knowing.

In the Rear-View Mirror

The highway of life is not always smooth;
too often it's rough and so hard to steer
over unpaved paths when you hit a groove.
You look past your woes in the rear-view mirror.

The grueling lifestyle soon takes its toll
on the mind and the body, year after year;
where your spirit had been is a gaping hole.
You look at yourself in the rear-view mirror.

A new life begins under close scrutiny,
but you are worried and living in fear
that the day will come of sheer mutiny.
Your legacy follows in the rear-view mirror.

Now the end of life approaches quickly;
you want those dear to be once more near,
but no one will come. You are old and sickly.
The future looks just like the rear-view mirror.

Being is Becoming

If the process of constantly becoming as a
person is integral to our very being,
according to the 19th century philosopher,
Nietzsche, who believed the very same,
then your life is filled with evolutionary
milestones, each one worth revealing.

At times you may have thought that your
bipolar disorder had driven you insane,
but your ability to successfully reinvent yourself
showed your strength to overcome;
and the 19th century philosopher, Nietzsche,
believed in the very same.

In moments of weakness, to drugs and
alcohol you ultimately succumbed.
This led to loss of home and business, and your family's demise;
but your ability to successfully reinvent yourself
showed your strength to overcome.

You often said, don't trust an alcoholic,
for they will always tell you lies.
This takes a great deal of honesty and
committed reform on your part,
for in the past you lost your home, your business,
and you saw your family's demise.

It is never too late to change yourself when
it comes genuinely from the heart.
Our lives are far too short to harbor grudges and negative feelings.
This takes a great deal of honesty and
committed reform on your part.

Every positive gesture made can only
facilitate the process of healing.
Our lives are far too short to harbor grudges and negative feelings.
If the process of constantly becoming as a
person is integral to our very being,
then your life is filled with evolutionary
milestones, each one worth revealing.

Silver Lining

You face overwhelming, chronic pain, to
which you are not resigning,
despite the many side effects of well-known therapies,
for time and toil have taught you well to look for the silver lining.

Explaining the illness to those without
may sound a lot like whining,
but true empathy only comes, it seems, from
those concerned with remedies.
You face overwhelming, chronic pain, to
which you are not resigning.

The losses you suffer are numerous; your heart, it must be pining
to face every day with uncertainty, yet you deal with maladies,
for time and toil have taught you well to look for the silver lining.

So many friendships come and go – you
could be out wining and dining!
However, family always comes first, you
have set your solid priorities.
You face overwhelming, chronic pain, to
which you are not resigning.

There was a time when all was well, and
the sun was forever shining,

but dark clouds formed and ushered in a storm of tragedies -
yet time and toil have taught you well to look for the silver lining.

Now change is the only constant, and the stars are re-aligning,
while nature dances playfully to the sounds of a new melody.
You face overwhelming, chronic pain, to
which you are not resigning,
for time and toil have taught you well to look for the silver lining.

My Drug Is True

My drug is Freedom.
Freedom from pain, freedom from fear,
freedom from all of the faults of myself,
freedom from the madness of this world,
freedom from any misgivings of this life.
My drug is Freedom, my drug is True.

My drug is Poetry.
Words on a page in poetic rhyme,
prosaic verse transcends space and time,
universal truths of the human kind
that expose emotion and expand your mind.
My drug is Poetry, my drug is True.

My drug is Love.
Hearts aglow in gentle reprieve,
fiery passion in heated seduction,
loss of loved ones that cause us to grieve,
maternal attachment of born reproduction.
My drug is Love. My drug is True.

How about You?

For Still She Waves

It all started to honor the fallen of our nation
in memorial after the Civil War.
The death count on both sides was so monumental
that bereaving mothers gathered as sisters in arms
to sort out the brothers by colors of blue and gray.

Since the First Memorial Day in our history
our laws stated that all people are created equally.
For what we stand, for what we believe,
for what we work, for what we receive,
for heroes, sheroes, and home of the brave,
for Stars and Stripes,
for still She waves.

Thank You for Sharing

The most difficult truths are so hard to express,
especially when they must be said to a loved one.
How often we struggle to find the right words,
and the best place and time to sit down and talk.

Whenever your friends are in a tight spot,
you offer clarity to the situation.
With practicality as a measuring stick,
you look to the future for best outcomes.

You always have such terrific advice,
and you seem to know just how to say things.
Your compassion is unsurpassed by none,
and experience has made you wise and strong.

For all of your guidance and worldly counsel,
I am grateful, and sincerely thank you for sharing.

Sands of Tim

Two hearts as one reunited in an airport -
seems we are destined to repeat these very roles.
No telling how or when the next chapter begins -
only revealed by the trickling sands of time.

You say Atlantic Shore, and we walk along the beach
to the roar of the incoming tide at mid-day;
my feet sink in sand, leaving fleeting impressions
as the waves rush to claim and deposit more shells.

They look young and strong as we did not long ago;
their wits and degrees will surely take them farther.
Together we must support their life-long learning
to ensure their success in a sandpaper world.

Full moon rises gold against blue sky in April.
Lonely loon croons a nocturnal lullaby.
Groups of geckos gather beneath the Melbourne moon
while a Chihuahua family bids me farewell.

What if Jesus Flew for United?

What if Jesus flew for United?
- escorting only the worthy souls
on a one-way trip for those invited.

The old and sick become excited,
shirking age and all its tolls.
What if Jesus flew for United?

When innocents remain delighted,
free from goals like wild foals,
on a one-way trip for those invited.

For all the lovers unrequited,
mending riddled hearts of holes,
what if Jesus flew for United?

Standing open, self-indicted;
waiting line, a hot bed of coals,
on a one-way trip for those invited.

Never hurts to be far-sighted,
slipping in among the trolls.
What if Jesus flew for United
on a one-way trip for those invited?

Empty Nest

The birds will take flight, leaving behind an empty nest,
as they prepare for the journey on their mass migration;
while the seasons must change, laying winter forever to rest.

Once there was a time they would mock each other in jest
with fantastic ideas about their future aspirations.
The birds will take flight, leaving behind an empty nest.

It reminds us of the days when we started our own quest,
and they watched us soar to heights of our own ambitions.
Still, the seasons must change, laying winter forever to rest.

The blessing of our children is intense as one would guess,
and to be without them so abruptly is a total interruption.
The birds will take flight, leaving behind an empty nest.

So many times, the elders would be with us as our guests,
and we will always hold them close with memories of adoration,
yet the seasons must change, laying winter forever to rest.

Now we've said our long farewells to our fathers-who-knew-best,
and we pray the young well with their higher educations.
The birds will take flight, leaving behind an empty nest,
while the seasons must change, laying winter forever to rest.

I Remembered

I remembered right away
that you promised not to go
without telling me about
your prior lives.

I remembered yesterday
we were packing for a trip
and our lovely holiday
at the sea shore.

I remembered as I slept
how you held me in your arms
and I felt so warm and safe
with you beside me.

I remembered when I wept
that you weren't coming back
and I felt so all alone
without you here.

I remembered that I lied
when I said I'll be just fine
but I wasn't very strong
in the long run.

Shari Jo LeKane

I remembered when I died
that we'd reunite one day
in a very different place
for all eternity.

I remembered no regret
having met you as we did
we were both so very young
but we were happy.

I remembered to forget
imperfections and mistakes
and to focus on the love
we made together.

Cinderella

She entered the ballroom to a lilting waltz
as he crossed the floor and extended a hand
to find her perfect and completely without fault

as the music was played by an orchestral band.
While the stepmother sucked on her cigarette
and the stepsisters oinked their droll demands,

they danced away in harmonious silhouette
only to forget about the very place and time.
Yet never once would either regret

the magical feelings that were so sublime
as they drifted beyond the ballroom site
and into a twilight, oh, so very divine,

when a magical kiss made them one that fine night
to fulfill what could have been only a dream;
until the clock rocked their world at the stroke of midnight,

when she parted her lips and then stifled a scream,
as she faded from sight like a wilting moonbeam.

The Prince Is Having A Ball

Notices flew through the click of the mouse
and they rushed to make plush everything for the ball.
Hands-on support came from every house

as they shared and prepared to restore the Great Hall.
Beautiful women lined up by the score.
Each was more lovely than one could recall.

Managed by cell phones, enhancers and more,
life for the plastics was displaced, surreal,
which made the selection for Prince quite a chore.

Simplistic confidence stole his appeal -
he escorted young miss to the back of the Castle
where under the moonlight they danced and revealed

a mutual passion without any hassle.
He kissed her so sweetly, she fell for this fella.
A thunderbolt clapped as she left him her tassel.

Lightly the raindrops fell from her umbrella
as Prince watched his retreating love, Cinderella.

Autumnal Equinox

The sun slips south on Summer's golden locks,
as nighttime boasts a glowing harvest moon;
transition to Autumnal Equinox.

Party boats are brought up onto the docks;
seems all too soon we put them out in June.
The sun slips south on Summer's golden locks.

Changing leaves contrast against the rocks,
while crisp, blue skies are high with hot air balloons;
transition to Autumnal Equinox.

Jazz at the Bistro and Friday night jocks,
song in the woods of a lonely loon croons.
The sun slips south on Summer's golden locks.

End Daylight Savings Time with every tic-toc;
evening waning just hours past noon;
transition to Autumnal Equinox.

Warm socks and sweaters as winter's door knocks;
until then we fall to a tender tune.
The sun slips south on Summer's golden locks;
transition to Autumnal Equinox.

Only in October

The Hunter's Moon shines only in October
when harvest is at end and fields are at rest;
then fox and hound in game must be sober.

In town, the farmers' market shows the best
of every pumpkin, mum and garden produce,
with beer and brats to start the October Fest.

The Clydesdales line up tethered by the noose
and pull the local ethnic polka band
with dairy queens in tow on the caboose.

A Shakespeare troupe performs at the Grand Stand
and weavers' guilds display their artful skill,
while craftsmen and quilters reveal their hand.

The sun is warm, but evening brings a chill;
a perfect time to join the polka dance,
or a frenzied fox-trot, or a waltzing thrill.

Romantic vistas are at every stance;
only in October does one get this chance.

Starry Night

Jupiter plays catch-up to the shiny Christmas Moon;
North Star of Big Dipper glows exceptionally bright;
signs this starry night that winter is coming soon.

Houses stand illuminated by sparkling holiday lights
surrounded in velvet darkness so quick and so cold.
North Star of Big Dipper glows exceptionally bright.

Events of this holiday season inevitably unfold.
Steal a sweet kiss from me under the mistletoe
surrounded in velvet darkness so quick and so cold.

Point to the sky because you wanted to show
how the night sky in winter has beautiful stars;
Steal a sweet kiss from me under the mistletoe.

It is hard to fathom eternity, or a light year so far.
Constellations, you say, are forever in motion,
and the night sky in winter has beautiful stars.

Celestial heavens are like a giant, spatial ocean,
and constellations, you say, are forever in motion.
Jupiter plays catch-up to the shiny, Christmas Moon,
signs this starry night that winter is coming soon.

Holy Night

A luminous star shone miraculous light
upon the Christ child asleep in the fold,
with animals speaking of peace at midnight.

Was born in a manger protected from cold.
Adored Holy Family, heavenly sight!
See the Christ child asleep in the fold!

Shepherds attracted to vision so bright:
the birth of our Savior as had been foretold.
Adored Holy Family, heavenly sight!

A star in the sky with a tail long and bold;
the sign traveled far and reached Kings of great might.
The birth of our Savior as had been foretold.

A tail in the sky is as long as a kite!
They came bearing gifts of strange spices and gold.
The sign traveled far and reached Kings of great might.

On this Holy Night all the righteous uphold!
They came bearing gifts of strange spices and gold.
A luminous star shone miraculous light,
with animals speaking of peace at midnight.

Dance of the Boughs

The forest is full of those tall, sacred vows,
when blue spruce in winter become Christmas trees
as snow and wind celebrate dance of the boughs.

At home on the farm with the horses and cows,
they roam in the fields and the wood properties.
The forest is full of those tall, sacred vows.

Corn has been harvested, turned by the plow,
and fields will lie fallow until the spring breeze
as snow and wind celebrate dance of the boughs.

The hunters and dogs, they attempt to arouse
wild game from their hiding for dinner to please.
The forest is full of those tall, sacred vows.

They gather a cord for the fireplace now,
and scavenge what deadwood the forest concedes
as snow and wind celebrate dance of the boughs.

A beautiful scene at the farm house, and how! -
while Christmas moon sparkles on all eyes can see.
The forest is full of those tall, sacred vows
as snow and wind celebrate dance of the boughs.

Wintery Silence

As twilight ascended in tender turquoise,
sleet fell like quicksilver running in vain
down the ebony trees that could shout without noise
in the wintery silence of country urbane.

Your boots kicked the shadows of puddles and cracks.
The bar was not far from where you parked your car.
I watched from the window with interest, tracking
your every move in the absence of stars.

When I walked in the door, you were shooting some pool
with a couple of females, aged 20 or so.
Then our eyes first met – very familiar, yet cool -
a distant attraction from so long ago.

I waited out back for hours in darkness,
as the frozen mix turned into powdery snow.
You brought them out drunk, and they laughed at the starkness
of feeling no cold despite temperatures low.

So deftly you wooed them to play in your hand;
insisted on giving them each a ride home.
Intrigued with the thought of a one-night stand,
they poured in the back seat by light of the dome.

FALL TENDERLY

I flew to your side and with wet, bated breath,
whispered my pleas in your white, jeweled ear;
climbed in the front where I settled like death
in the wintery silence that pierced the night's fear.

The ride to your man cave was broken by quivers
and trembling limbs huddled in the back seat.
I stared in arousal at visible shivers;
they sat very close in the absence of heat.

The path ended somewhere in back of the woods
at a single log cabin; we gathered within.
And there by the door, a stuffed grizzly bear stood
as he beckoned we enter and feasting begin.

You chose her so quickly, her beauty entrancing,
the music was playing, you poured her a drink.
I moved to the other, we all started dancing,
the mood was romantic, so close to the brink.

My mind started swirling, twirling, whirling -
the room was a virtual merry-go-round;
I took one more drink from the wine – I was hurling
before I fell face-down and lay on the ground.

You spoke to the other as if I were dead;
it never once threatened the smile on your face.
The two of you whispered *come hither* instead,
and welcomed her into your friendly embrace.

Knotty pine walls made a beautiful pattern,
reflecting the fireplace, soft and warm glow.
Full moon in orbit with Jupiter, Saturn -
a wintery silence upon the fresh snow.

Shari Jo LeKane

Grizzly bear rests in a heap on the floor,
(seems he was standing when we first arrived).
A wet trail of blood led me past the front door
to the stifling darkness that helped me revive.

Your entrails were lashed about, strewn from the tree
where your body hung limp as a withered balloon.
Puncture marks stood out so plainly to see
that the prime of your life drained away all too soon.

No sign of the car or of any live soul,
only the hoot of an old screechy owl
who witnessed calamity in this hell hole;
I looked at the moon and let out a strange howl.

Already naked, I feared no great shame.
The dampness of fur was so sickeningly sweet
with the smell of blood and the taste of game.
I needed a shower (wash, rinse, repeat).

The dawn sprinkled stars in a early red morning.
I covered your body with shovels of dirt
then headed to town like a storm without warning
wearing your jacket, your pants and silk shirt.

When I walked in the door they were shooting some pool -
a couple of females, aged 20 or so.
Then our eyes first met – very familiar, yet cool -
a distant attraction from not long ago....

Perpetual Motion

Like endless waves upon the sea,
my thoughts are in perpetual motion
seeking out the depths of me
in caverns of a bottomless ocean,
mysterious and full of notions.

If kisses start a broken heart,
then action begets motivation.
Two star-crossed lovers cannot part,
attraction of the constellations.
Synergy made of recreation.

The wheat, the chaff and the weevil
are a juggle and desensitize;
the struggle between good and evil
turns a view from hypnotic surprise
to a vision that is tenured and wise.

With gift of life comes curse of death.
We nurse existential needs to the hearse
and celebrate a life's last breath.
Perpetual motion for better or worse,
a microcosm of the universe.

Once in a Blue Moon

Once in a blue moon the gray wolf emerges
refined from his former lycanthropic craze.
Gracefully bridling animal urges
with lyrical language, he catches my gaze.

Like staring down truth after lightning strikes twice,
his eyes walk the back streets of my broken heart.
We drink to eternity in paradise
and he needles a whisper that we'll never part.

Wandering aimlessly, corners so narrow,
the darkness enfolding in our space alone.
Kisses so sharp that they pierce like an arrow
while biting the loneliness deep in my bones.

Moaning, I strengthen and stifle a howl.
We run through the thicket. "Who-Who?" knows the owl.

Monarch

They gathered softly in a field for many miles around
to taste in haste the flowers before showers tumbled down
upon the clover blooms, the goldenrod, thistles and grasses;
never in one place too long as hungry blackbird passes.

An undulating wave of black and orange fills the skies.
Silent as a fairy, painted masterpiece that flies
on wings so paper thin, who could begin to realize
the journey and the magnitude for creatures of their size.

Locations to migrate are as innate as procreation.
From Canada to Mexico and through our very nation,
the Monarch is a royal, truly loyal to its subjects
in all of North America; to this, no one objects.

So, when I see the King float on his wings alone and stray,
just nosing in my garden on a lazy summer day,
I know he's on hiatus as a weary renegade,
for somewhere on their journey flies the whole Monarch Brigade.

Double Exposure

Life in the darkness, by quirk or design,
where colors are silver and black is a blight,
and infinite lines are reverse realigned.

No diff'rence from midday to stroke of midnight.
Despite chains that bind, the reveries unwind
where colors are silver and black is a blight.

Warts on my mind that explode from behind,
the memories fester long into the night.
Despite chains that bind, the reveries unwind.

Far flights of freedom to frightening heights!
And then I went blind which could not be defined.
the memories fester long into the night.

My daily grind is good deeds done in kind.
I live in the moment way-the-hell out of sight.
And then I went blind which could not be defined.

The deck threw me double exposure, alright.
I live in the moment way-the-hell out of sight.
Life in the darkness, by quirk or design,
and infinite lines are reverse realigned.

February

February brings
loneliness of pioneers
but I'm close to you

Bitter winter sting
groundhog comes out from below
shadow dark and blue

Icicles melting
liquid to the winter sun
frozen to the moon

Valentine sending
wishes from a loving heart
Cupid's arrow flew

British invading
She loves you ya ya ya ya
yesterday so soon

Orchid show viewing
lady slipper's spotted silk
perfect purple bloom

Shari Jo LeKane

Four score and counting
presidential holiday
founding fathers true

Rosa was sitting
we shall overcome someday
all stand equal too

Springtime impending
sprouting just beneath the snow
flowers will march through

Doldrums

These are the dark days
with long lonely nights
and frozen starlight,
the full moon so bright,
of tar paper prison by electric candlelight.

These are the dark days
when you're not quite right,
not any longer,
you're not feeling stronger,
you don't even belong here,
there is something so wrong here,
the sun is gone, clearly
it makes you feel weary
the promise of solstice
seems utterly hopeless
and spring equinox
should be next on the clocks.

These dark, dark days
will get longer, my friend,
day by day, minute by minute,
winter doldrums will end.
Meanwhile, I will dance
with the doldrums to send
them off, until they completely disappear.

The Lorax on Westgate

An educated gentleman named David C. Howard
set about the business of saving some trees,
and before long became known as the local Lorax
for his ability to represent the masses and please
the citizenry for saving the treasured memories
in those trees that the "agencies" tried so hard to seize.

The truth is that beauty is relative to what one sees,
and no one knows this more than David C. Howard;
but the accumulation of collective community memories
surrounded generations of those multiple, particular trees.
So someone had to petition to hear the sordid pleas
of the trees under siege; hence, the rise of the Lorax.

The case became know internally at H.Q. as "Code Lorax,"
and the idea was to get the clear-cutting to cease
along the South Park Greenway, whose canopy was so pleasing,
as noted by those represented by the Lorax, a.k.a. "Howard,"
who spoke for the residents along Westgate, and the trees,
and who desperately guarded those historical memories.

What started as an idea of only three people, in memory,
began to decoalesce because of due diligence of the Lorax,
who took on the agencies and spoke for the trees.
He appeared before committees with his own arborist, "who sees

FALL TENDERLY

that the trees have a life and a right," so says Howard,
"to continue to thrive and provide what has and will always please."

The campaign gained momentum as many
neighbors voiced their pleas
in the face of various committees and before
a forester with foggy memories;
but perseverance prevailed, and no one knows just how hard
the work and commitment sustained the
vision of "The Lone Lorax."
He knew the Sweetgums should stay, providing
shade, and so much more, as he sees,
for utility usurps aesthetics in this debate
over clear-cutting the trees!

And so an edict came from City Hall to
the committees about the trees
asking each of them specifically to pay
attention, if they would, please,
to consider the proposal at hand, with or
without modifications, and then cease
to consider it furthermore, but to eradicate it from their memories
once their recommendations have been made,
and the Council will deal with the Lorax,
and therefore, approve or disapprove the matter
in session, and before David C. Howard.

However, notice came down from City Hall conceding
the project, so that the trees and the memories
along South Park Greenway were ultimately saved,
which immensely pleased The Lone Lorax,
and oh, so many more, who see them now, and will
see them later, smiles a proud Mr. Howard!

Spring Equinox

The blanket of darkness releases its hold,
in anticipation from winter to spring,
while each passing minute thaws into the light
revealing its slumbering secrets.

Such vulnerability merits respect,
for surely these tenuous moments in time
of sweet, gentle blossoms and soft, tender shoots
are subject to weathery perils.

Transitional focus brings strange ironies
across snowy gardens all newly exposed.
So raw are the changes, a new destiny
to be found in this fresh transformation.

Miraculous season, the Spring Equinox -
return of the bright, all her colors reborn
in a rainbow of flowers, and trees blooming full,
and the song of the birds and the bees.

About the Author

Shari Jo LeKane (B.A. English, Spanish; M.A. Spanish - Saint Louis University Madrid/St. Louis) lives in St. Louis, Missouri, writes articles, literary critiques, poetry and prose. She is a consultant for not-for-profit, business, community development, education, leadership development, disability, and elderly advocacy, and she teaches Spanish Language and Culture in a local university, and creative writing to men in a maximum-security jail and to special needs students.

She wrote a novel in verse, Poem to Follow, two books of poetry, Fall Tenderly and Surviving Gracefully, and is featured in several poetry anthologies, including the Missouri VSA 2013 Anthology, Turning the Clocks Forward Again; Poetica Victorian; Red Dashboard Disorder Anthology: Mental Illness and Its Effects; Think Pink; The Muse India/Createspace Anthology Of Present Day Best Poems (Vols. I, II, III & IV); Bordertown Press Poetry of People on the Move; The Society of Classical Poets (Vol. I, VI); The Mas Tequila Review; Snapping Twig; The Lonely Crowd; Form Quarterly; Devolution Z; The Quarterday Review; Adelaide Literary Magazine; Adelaide Literary Awards Poetry Finalist Best of 2017 Anthology; Adelaide Voices Literary Award for Poetry Shortlist Winner for 2018; MacroMicroCosm Literary and Arts Review: Solstice; The Road Not Taken; The Faircloth Review; Bindweed; Halcyon Days; Lunaris Review; Iconoclast; The Poeming Pigeon; Unrequited: An Anthology of Love Poems about Inanimate Objects; and Literature Today International Journal of Contemporary Literature (Vols. I, II, & VI). Shari's poetry has been published in several literary magazines in the U.S., Canada, England, India, Ireland, Nigeria, Portugal, Scotland, Spain and Wales, and she has been featured in spoken word on the award-winning CD, 'How Live?' with LOOPRAT. Shari considers herself a modern formalist, addressing contemporary issues in poetic verse with a stylized language.

Acknowledgements

This book of poetry is dedicated with love to those who suffer and find relief through artistic expression.

Acromegaly (akrōˈmegəlē) – also known as adult gigantism – is a debilitating disease caused by overproduction of growth hormone due to a pituitary tumor. In 2009 I was diagnosed and had brain surgery and gamma knife laser surgery to remove as much of the tumor as possible. For two years I was completely dysfunctional, and unable to read, write or concentrate due to chronic pain and highly elevated growth hormone levels. I grew from 130 lbs. to 210 lbs. (from a size 8 to a size 18).

I began listening to various meditation tapes to relieve stress, and *The Mayo Clinic Guide To Pain Relief* proved to be the most enlightening clinical literature I came across for chronic pain, thanks to my dear friend, Elsie Frances Johnson.

Another study that broadened my scope on redeveloping the brain functioning came from Exeter University, *Poetry is Like Music to the Mind, Scientists Prove*. When volunteers read one of their favorite passages of poetry, the team found that "areas of the brain associated with memory were stimulated more strongly than 'reading areas', indicating that reading a favorite passage is a kind of recollection. In a specific comparison between poetry and prose, the team found evidence that poetry activates brain areas, such as the posterior cingulate cortex and medial temporal lobes, which have been linked to introspection."

In 2011, I was invited to teach creative writing at the local county jail with a dear friend, Jane Ellen Ibur, and it has literally saved my life. Between working with the students in the jail and writing for myself, which has become an important part of my lifestyle, I have managed to recover a great part of my socio-linguistic skills and creative writing capabilities that I believed were forever lost to me.

I was also very fortunate that my employer worked with me from the very beginning to help me gradually reintegrate into the work environment, albeit on a part-time basis. Nonetheless, were it not for their patience and willingness to work with me, I would not have recovered my cognitive skills and abstract thinking capacities. To this day, I continue to develop my skills with professional certifications and licenses through online courses and classes.

In 2016, I was invited to participate in a worldwide acromegaly study to get a new drug approved through the FDA that controls the growth hormone without the negative side effects of the cancer shots. I am forever indebted to the team of doctors and nurses at Washington University Medical Center, Barnes Jewish Hospital, and throughout St. Louis, Missouri who continue to work with me on a regular basis to manage my disease and conditions so that I may lead a fulfilling life.

My eternal thanks go to The St. Vincent de Paul Society and to Betsy Grant for her eternal support, to All Saint Church, and to the Choir with whom I sing for their spiritual enlightenment.

I also thank Dr. Victoria Gonzalez-Rubio for providing me endless reading material, encouragement and inspiration throughout me recovery.

I truly thank my mother, without whom, I could not have survived this ordeal, and for always being there when I need her. And I thank my children with love for always sticking by my side.

Publishing Credits

"Fall Tenderly" was first featured in *HIP Literary Magazine* in December 2012, in *Tuck Magazine* in January 2013, on the Apple Tree/The Screech Owl in October 2014, in *Think Pink* Issue #1 in January 2015, and in *The Quarterday Review* of November 2015.

"Starry Night" first appeared in *HIP Literary Magazine* in December 2012, in *Poetica Victorian* in January 2014, and in *Halcyon Days* in December 2016.

"Midnight Affair" first appeared in *Tuck Magazine* in July 2014, later in *The Apple Tree/The Screech Owl* in October 2014, in *Think Pink* Issue #1 of January 2015, in *The Mas Tequila Review* of March 2015, in *Form Quarterly* of July 2015, and in *The Road Not Taken* published in April 2016.

"I Remembered" was featured with other poetry in *Adelaide Literary Magazine* in February 2017.

"Perpetual Motion" appeared in *The Lunaris Review* in April 2016.

"Wedding Vow" was published in *Literature Today Volume II* in January 2015.

"After Dark" was featured with other poems in *Think Pink* Issue #1 in January 2015.

"I Am Woman" was published by Magdalena Biela in January of 2015.

"Monarch" appeared on *The Society of Classical Poets* in February 2015.

"Spring Equinox" was published by *Snapping Twig* in March 2015, by *Every Writer's Everyday Poems* in April 2017, and by *Miracle Magazine Rebirth Issue* in June 2017.

"Double Exposure" was featured in *Contemporary Poetry Volume II An Anthology of Present Day Best Poems* in October 2015.

"Have You Seen My Gray Today?" was published in The Muse India's *Anthology of Present Best Day Poems 2014* and was featured on *Every Writer's Resource/Everyday Poems* in October 2014.

"Timekeeper's Waltz" first appeared in *Tuck Magazine* in July 2014 and later in the *The Apple Tree/The Screech Owl* in October 2014.

"Pain" and "Harmonious Mix" were featured in *The Apple Tree/The Screech Owl* in September and October 2014 respectively.

"What If Jesus Flew for United" was published in Bordertown Press' *Poetry of People on the Move* in September 2014.

"Autumnal Equinox" appeared in *Literature Today, An International Journal of Contemporary Literature* in September 2014 and in *MacroMicroCosm Literary Art Journal: Solstice* in January 2016.

"You Cannot Live Here Anymore" and "The Bitter to The Sweet" debuted in Red Dashboard's *Disorder Anthology: "Mental Illness and Its Effects"* in April 2014. "You Cannot Live Here Anymore" later appeared in *and/or* Volume 4 in June 2014.

"Farewell Miss Saigon" appeared in *Silver Apples Magazine* in April 2014.

"Desert with No End" was published in *Ancient Paths Literary Magazine* in January 2014.

"Sands of Time" was printed in *Manic Fervor* "The Mad Hatter" in January 2014.

"Pearls of Wisdom" was published by Magdalena Biela in August 2013, later by *Think Pink Issue #1* in January 2015, and in *Contemporary Poetry Volume Three: An Anthology of Present Day Best Poems* published in January 2017.

"Wintery Silence" first appeared in *Niteblade* in December of 2013 and later in *Devolution Z Magazine* in August of 2015.

"My Disease" was featured in the Missouri VSA Anthology, *Turning the Clocks Forward Again* in 2013.

"The Humanitarian" was published in *Poetica Victorian* in October 2013.

"Hang" was printed in *Miracle Ezine Magazine* in October 2013 and by *The Poet's Haven* in November 2013.

"My Drug is True" appeared in *Coffeeshop Poems* in December 2012.

www.ingramcontent.com/pod-product-compliance
Lightning Source LLC
Chambersburg PA
CBHW020238090426
42735CB00010B/1748